Wile E. Coyote

Experiments with
SIMPLE MACHINES

by
Mark Weakland

illustrated by
Christian Cornia

SMASH!!

CAPSTONE PRESS
a capstone imprint

Published in 2014 by Capstone Press
A Capstone Imprint
1710 Roe Crest Drive
North Mankato, Minnesota 56003
www.capstonepub.com

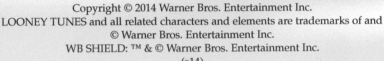

Library of Congress Cataloging-in-Publication Data
Weakland, Mark, author.
Smash! : Wile E. Coyote experiments with simple machines / by Mark Weakland;
illustrated by Christian Cornia.
pages cm.—(Warner Brothers. Wile E. Coyote, physical science genius)
Summary: "Uses popular cartoon character Wile E. Coyote to demonstrate
science concepts involved with simple machines."—Provided by publisher.
Audience: Ages 10-12.
Audience: Grades 4 to 6.
Includes bibliographical references and index.
ISBN 978-1-4765-4222-5 (library binding)
ISBN 978-1-4765-5213-2 (paperback)
1. Simple machines—Juvenile literature. 2. Simple machines—Experiments—Juvenile literature.
3. Science projects—Juvenile literature. 4. Wile E. Coyote (Fictitious character)—Juvenile
literature. I. Warner Bros. II. Title. III. Title: Wile E. Coyote experiments with simple machines.
IV. Title: Experiments with simple machines.
TJ147.W397 2014
621.8'11—dc23   2013037017

Editorial Credits
Aaron Sautter, editor; Lori Bye, designer; Laura Manthe, production specialist

Cover Artist: Andrés Martínez Ricci

Capstone Press thanks Joanne K. Olson, Associate Professor of Science Education at
Iowa State University for her help in creating this book.

Printed in the United States   3679

Table of Contents

Introduction:

A Better Way to Work

Catching a Road Runner is hard work. There are rocks to move, anvils to lift, and holes to dig. But no matter how hard Wile E. Coyote works, he never manages to catch that crafty bird. Wile E. wouldn't have to work so hard if he learned to correctly use simple machines. The six types of simple machines include levers, wheels and axles, pulleys, inclined planes, wedges, and screws.

Road Runner

(Speedius birdius)

When Wile E. exerts a force to lift a rock or dig a hole, he does work. In science, work is defined as the effort or force needed to move an object over a certain distance. Using simple machines would make Wile E.'s work much easier. Why? Because simple machines reduce the amount of force he needs to move something. If he pushed a lever or pulled a rope on a pulley, the same work would be done with a lot less force. Learn how to use simple machines, Wile E.! Your work will be easier, and you might have more luck catching Road Runner too!

anvil—a large steel block with a flat top

Coyote

(Hungrius carnivorii)

Chapter 1: Whatever the Lever

Levers and Fulcrums

A deep pit makes a good Road Runner trap. But digging is hard work. And Wile E. isn't strong enough to lift a big stone out of his hole.

A simple lever can help Wile E. solve his problem. A lever is a bar that turns against a resting point called a **fulcrum**. To make a lever, Wile E. first jams one end of a pry bar under the big rock. Then he places a smaller rock under the bar to be the fulcrum.

With the lever, Wile E. can lift a heavy **load** like the big rock with much less effort. But he needs to place the fulcrum in the correct spot. If it's too close to him, the lever moves only a short distance when he pushes on it. It barely affects the rock.

But if Wile E. places the fulcrum closer to the big rock, the lever moves over a greater distance. This creates a large force on the other end of the pry bar. But be careful, Wile E.! If you exert too much force, it can lead to unexpected—and painful—results!

fulcrum—a resting point on which a lever pivots
load—an object that moves when a force is applied

Input and Output Forces

Wile E. has learned that flying rocks can be hard on the head. Now he'd like to launch a boulder at Road Runner. But how can he throw it accurately? His ACME catapult should get the job done!

Wile E.'s catapult is a lever made with a sturdy bar and a fulcrum. Like all levers, it involves two separate forces. An input force is applied to the lever to move a load. The output force is the result of the lever acting on the load. For example, a strong spring provides input force on the catapult's arm, which turns on a fulcrum. This results in a strong output force that launches the boulder through the air.

WHUMP!

What Wile E. doesn't know is that sometimes an output force from one system can act as an input force for another. When his catapult flings the boulder, it causes another to come hurtling back at him. Look out, Wile E.!

OUCH!

Chapter 2: Inclined to Fail

Planes and Ramps

Looks like Wile E. still plans to crush Road Runner with a heavy object. But he's having trouble getting that big log to the top of the canyon wall. Luckily for him, there's more than one way to move a heavy object.

A plane is any flat surface, such as a smooth board lying flat on the ground. Unfortunately, a flat plane isn't very useful for making work easier. However, Wile E. can create a simple machine by lifting one end of the plane. Like other simple machines, inclined planes reduce the effort needed to move a heavy load.

RAMP

LOG

ME

Wile E. doesn't need to lift the log up a short distance. Instead, he can simply roll it up a ramp, which is a type of inclined plane. The ramp allows Wile E. to exert a smaller force over a longer distance. The result is the same—the heavy log moves to a new height. Only this time Wile E. doesn't have to work as hard.

CRASH!

Of course, it would have been better if he had built his ramp strong enough to support the log's weight!

Moving from High to Low

Can a coyote catch a roadrunner with a ski jump?
Wile E. thinks so, and he's about to find out!

Inclined planes are useful for moving something
from a low point to a high point. But they also help
do the opposite. Wile E.'s ski jump quickly moves him
from a high point to a low point. If he uses it correctly,
he should easily catch Road Runner.

SMAK!

But Wile E. should also remember that the force of gravity constantly pulls objects toward the ground. Gravity quickly pulls loose objects down a ramp.

Pulled by gravity, Wile E. zooms down the ramp. Uh, oh. It looks like Wile E. didn't think about how much gravity would affect him. Too much speed caused him to have too much distance on his jump. You overshot your target Wile E.!

gravity—a force that pulls objects with mass together

The Wedge

Wile E. has tried rolling logs and flinging boulders with catapults. But he hasn't had any luck in squashing Road Runner. He's got another idea to try, though. Maybe a rolling boulder will get the job done.

To release the boulder, Wile E. uses an axe to cut through a rope. An axe is a type of simple machine called a wedge. A wedge is made of two inclined planes that come together to a point on one side. Wedges are usually made of a strong material like wood or steel. Doorstops, chisels, and axes are all examples of wedges.

Like all simple machines, wedges do work. Their pointed ends can enter tight places and are good for pushing things apart. Doorstops can prop open doors. Chisels can split apart stone and cement. And axes are good at chopping through rope and wood.

After cutting the rope, Wile E. sees that a cactus is in the way. So he uses his wedge-shaped axe to chop it down. Unfortunately, he didn't think to place some other wedges under the boulder first. They could have kept the boulder from flattening him!

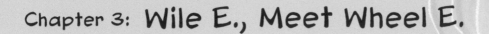

Chapter 3: Wile E., Meet Wheel E.

Rotational Motion of Wheels and Axles

Wile E.'s efforts have given him a headache instead of a tasty dinner. But he's hoping his wheeled wagon will provide a less painful way to squash that pesky Road Runner.

A wheel and axle is a simple machine that produces **rotational motion.** This motion can be used for doing work, such as moving heavy boulders. Wile E.'s wagon rests on top of two axles. When he pushes on it, the wheels turn and the wagon moves, along with anything sitting on it.

WHEEL

AXLE

Wheels and axles are simple machines that make life easier for everyone, including coyotes. With his wheeled wagon, Wile E. can move a giant boulder with just a push of his paw. However, wagons and boulders weigh a lot, and some rock ledges aren't very strong. Poor Wile E., here comes another headache!

CRACK!

rotational motion—the motion of an object rotating around a fixed point

Rotational vs. Straight-Line Motion

Wile E. has had trouble using a catapult and a wheeled vehicle by themselves. But what if he tried using them together? Armed with a catapult on a wagon, Wile E. sets out to crush Road Runner. He just has to get his machine into position. What could possibly go wrong?

Wheels and axles help create straight-line motion. When wheels are attached to vehicles, their rotational motion is transferred to the vehicles through the axles. This motion in turn causes the vehicles to move in a straight line. Any objects carried by the vehicles also move in a straight line. Wheeled vehicles can carry heavy loads in a straight line over long distances.

Of course, wheeled vehicles need to be kept under control. If they aren't, they can roll away and cause a lot of problems. Too bad Wile E. overlooked this fact. Now he's the one about to get crushed!

SPROING!

Chapter 4: Pull Me, Pull E.

The Pulley

To pull off his latest plan, Wile E. needs to get to the top of a platform. But how can he get himself up there? Using his scrawny arms and legs to climb up would be a lot of work. Why not use a simple machine like a pulley to do the job?

Pulleys are simple machines that make raising and lowering loads much easier. Wile E.'s pulley uses a rope and a grooved wheel. The wheel rotates around an axle. The rotational motion of the pulley causes the rope to move either up or down. Wile E. can use the wheel's motion to raise and lower objects, including himself.

A pulley makes work easier by changing the direction of force that Wile E. needs to apply to the rope. If he pulled up on a rope without a pulley, he'd be working against gravity. But if he uses a pulley, he can work with gravity instead. When he pulls down on one side, the other side moves up. Wile E.'s pulley can help him get to the top of the platform quickly and easily. But he didn't expect Road Runner to be at the top!

Reducing Applied Force

Dropping rocks from a high ledge hasn't worked well for Wile E. This time he thinks an anvil might work better. But pulling an anvil up to the top of a ledge is difficult. Wile E. knows that a pulley can help lift objects. Unfortunately, one pulley isn't enough to get his heavy anvil up to the rock ledge. What if he tries using more than one?

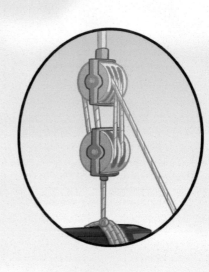

Using multiple pulleys makes work easier because they reduce the force needed to lift heavy objects. If Wile E. uses two pulleys, he can use half as much force to lift the anvil. Using three pulleys would reduce his effort to one-third of what he needed before. And with four pulleys, Wile E. would need to use just one-fourth of the force.

However, applied forces and distance always balance out. Pulleys greatly reduce the amount of force Wile E. uses to lift the anvil. But he has to pull a lot more rope to achieve his goal.

Oops! Wile E. missed one small detail. He didn't need to keep walking backward with the rope. He could have stayed in one spot to hoist the anvil up. Looks like he'll be hanging around for a while until he figures out a new plan.

Chapter 5: Spiraling Out of Control

Screws

Wile E. hasn't had much luck so far. But he would still love to crush Road Runner under a big rock. His latest idea is to use a jack to do some heavy lifting for him.

Jacks are complex machines. But the main part of a jack is a simple machine called a screw. A screw is an inclined plane that is wrapped around a **cylinder**. Its spiraling edge is very useful for doing difficult tasks.

cylinder—a shape with flat, circular ends and sides shaped like a tube

Screws are usually used for holding things together, such as two pieces of wood or a lid on a jar. But screws are also useful for raising and lowering heavy objects. When the screw in a jack turns, a platform moves up or down along the screw's inclined plane.

While a screw can help make lifting objects easier, turning it can be difficult. Wile E. can make his job even easier by using a motor to turn the screw. But he's got to be careful! A motorized screw can get out of control. Wile E. should learn that sometimes it's better to just do the work by hand.

Screws Convert Rotational Motion

   Dropping anvils and boulders from a high ledge hasn't worked well for Wile E. So instead he's going to try dropping the ledge itself—by blasting it with dynamite! But first Wile E. needs to drill a hole into the rock to hold the explosives.

   Like wheels and axles, screws can change rotational motion into other types of motion. Augers are large motorized screws used for drilling holes into the earth. The rotational motion of the motor turns the auger. As the auger turns, its spiraling edges move it down into the rock. Soon the screw-shaped auger creates a hole.

Uh, oh! Looks like Wile E.'s machine got stuck on some extra hard rock. The motor's rotational motion was shifted to Wile E. instead of the auger. The fast spinning motion sent him flying over the cliff's edge. Sometimes nothing seems to go right, even for a "Super Genius" like Wile E.

Simple Machines to the Rescue

Wile E. hasn't had much success in getting Road Runner. But simple machines have played an important part in his schemes. From moving boulders to drilling holes, simple machines have helped Wile E. do a lot of work.

pulley

wheel and axle

screw

wedge

inclined plane

lever

Simple machines are important for other reasons too. More complicated machines are often made from combining simple machines. Bicycles and bulldozers use a combination of levers, wheels and axles, pulleys, and more. Without simple machines, many machines in our world would not exist. We wouldn't be able to build roads and buildings, drive cars, or explore space without the help of simple machines.

Will Wile E. ever be able to capture Road Runner? Only time will tell. Although he hasn't had much luck, he'll keep trying. If Wile E. ever catches that sneaky bird, chances are good that a simple machine will help him finally succeed.

Glossary

anvil (AN-vuhl)—a large steel block with a flat top

cylinder (SI-luhn-duhr)—a shape with flat, circular ends and sides shaped like a tube

fulcrum (FUL-kruhm)—a resting point on which a lever pivots

gravity (GRAV-uh-tee)—a force that pulls objects with mass together

load (LOHD)—an object that moves when a force is applied

rotational motion (roh-TAY-shun-uhl MO-shun)—the motion of an object rotating around a fixed point

Read More

Deane-Pratt, Ade. *Simple Machines.* How Things Work. New York: PowerKids Press, 2012.

Oxlade, Chris. *Simple Experiments with Wheels and Axles.* Science Experiments with Simple Machines. New York: Windmill Books, 2014.

Silverman, Buffy. *Simple Machines: Forces in Action.* Do It Yourself. Chicago: Heinemann Library, 2009.

Internet Sites

FactHound offers a safe, fun way to find Internet sites related to this book. All of the sites on FactHound have been researched by our staff.

Here's all you do:

Visit *www.facthound.com*

Type in this code: 9781476542225

 **Super-cool stuff!** Check out projects, games and lots more at **www.capstonekids.com**

Index